Eye

Written by Jo Windsor

Look at the spider.
Look at the eyes.

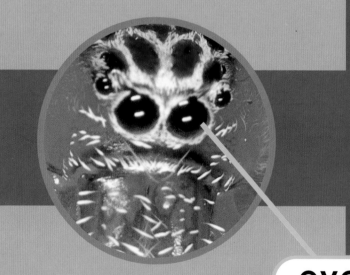

eye

3

Look at the dog.
Look at the eyes.

eye

4

Look at the fly.
Look at the eyes.

eye

Look at the owl.
Look at the eyes.

eye

Look at the frog.
Look at the eyes.

eye

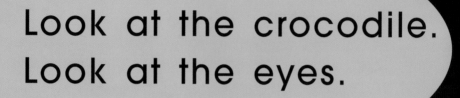

Look at the crocodile.
Look at the eyes.

eye

Index

▬▬ **Guide Notes**

Title: Eyes

Stage: Emergent – Magenta

Genre: Nonfiction (Expository)

Approach: Guided Reading

Processes: Thinking Critically, Exploring Language, Processing Information

Written and Visual Focus: Photographs (static images), Index, Labels

Word Count: 48

FORMING THE FOUNDATION

Tell the children that this book is about the different eyes that some animals have.
Talk to them about what is on the front cover. Read the title and the author.
Focus the children's attention on the index and talk about the different eyes
in this book.
"Walk" through the book, focusing on the photographs and talk about different eyes,
e.g., shape, size, and place on the body.

Read the text together.

THINKING CRITICALLY

(sample questions)

After the reading
*   What is the same about some of the animals' eyes and what is different?
*   Why do you think the eyes have to be where they are on the animals' body?

EXPLORING LANGUAGE

(ideas for selection)

Terminology
Title, cover, author, photographs

Vocabulary
Interest words: eyes, spider, dog, fly, owl, frog, crocodile
High-frequency words: look, at, the